What Do Cats Dream?

Also by Louise Rafkin and Illustrated by Alison Bechdel

What Do Dogs Dream?

What Do Cats Dream?

by Louise Rafkin
Illustrations by Alison Bechdel

**Andrews McMeel
Publishing**

Kansas City

www.andrewsmcmeel.com

99 00 01 02 03 KWF 10 9 8 7 6 5 4 3 2 1

ISBN: 0 8362 7872 0

Design by Holly Camerlinck

For Smokey and Sherlock

In my dream, I could work the can opener.

—Hans

WHAT DO CATS DREAM?

I was some sort of
poodle-cat—
so I didn't shed! It was
such a relief. Lately,
I make myself sneeze.

—Fluffy

WHAT DO CATS DREAM?

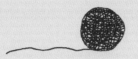

I was pregnant, and then
I gave birth to a kitten.
When I woke up I realized
I had thrown up a
hair ball in my sleep.

—Missy K.

The dog got blamed for everything.

—Blackie

My claws grew back,
but then they wouldn't
stop growing.

Spike (declawed)

In all my dreams,
dogs are the size of mice.

—Button

My litter box was
really big—
like the Sahara.

Jake

WHAT DO CATS DREAM?

That kid that tried to give me a bath? In my dream, he drowned.

—Giddy

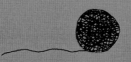

Everybody slept during the day and stayed up at night. At first it was fun, but then I began to feel really crowded.

— Julia

I got fixed!

—Diva Dinah
Queen of Sheba, champion Birman
and mother of fifty four

I dreamed of a velvet pillow and diamonds. When I woke up on the ratty sofa, I was so disappointed, I wept.

—Muffin (who prefers to be called Tiffany)

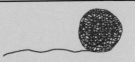

In the dream someone told me I was no longer cute. I keep hearing her say that Jinks used to be cute like me when he was a kitten. Now, I'm afraid to grow up.

—Jinks, Jr. (3 months old)

Th<u>ey</u> had to wear
stupid sweaters.

—Skinny-dipper (hairless)

I was licking the side of the bathtub, and then suddenly, I fell in!

—Eclaire

They pointed to the middle of the bed—right between them—and said.

"Come on up. Sweetie."

—Phoebe

It seems crazy, but I
went to someone else
to get groomed.

—Critter

I could reach right through the picture window!

— Bunkie

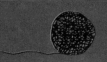

I got along with all the other cats in the neighborhood. Instead of cat fights, we got together for catnip parties.

— Kitty Cousteau

In the dream I knew some
fancy Bruce Lee moves.
That tom that
usually beats me up?
I nailed him.

—Pee-Wee

I dreamed I was sleeping.
It was a perfect dream.

—Misty